MAKER MODELS

SPACE CENTRE

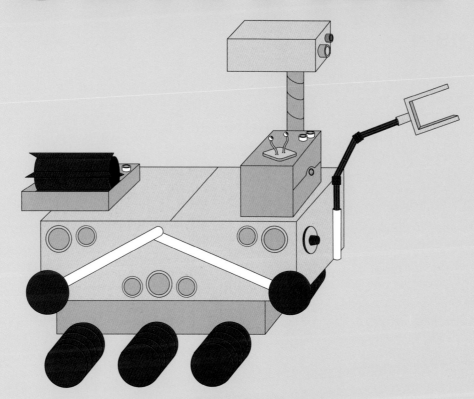

Anna Claybourne

WAYLAND
www.waylandbooks.co.uk

First published in Great Britain in 2019
by Wayland
Copyright © Hodder and Stoughton
All rights reserved

Editor: Elise Short
Design and illustration: Collaborate

HB ISBN 978 1 5263 0711 8
PB ISBN 978 1 5263 0712 5

Printed and bound in China

Wayland, an imprint of
Hachette Children's Group
Part of Hodder and Stoughton
Carmelite House
50 Victoria Embankment
London EC4Y 0DZ

An Hachette UK Company

www.hachette.co.uk
www.hachettechildrens.co.uk

The website addresses (URLs) included in this book were valid at the time of going to press. However, it is possible that contents or addresses may have changed since the publication of this book. No responsibility for any such changes can be accepted by either the author or the Publisher.

Note: In preparation of this book, all due care has been exercised with regard to the instructions, activities and techniques depicted. The publishers regret that they can accept no liability for any loss or injury sustained. Always get adult supervision and follow manufacturers' advice when using electric and battery-powered appliances.

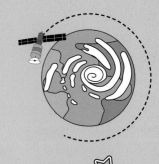

CONTENTS

REACH FOR THE STARS!

We have always been fascinated by the Sun and Moon, the stars and planets, and the night sky. We've invented rockets, rovers, satellites and space stations that allow us to leave Earth and explore the mysteries of space. We launch spacecraft from huge spaceports and space centres, where astronauts train and space scientists plan bold new missions.

If you're obsessed with all things space, this book is for you. It shows you how to make models of all kinds of spacecraft and space gear, along with a space centre to keep them in. You can do all this using everyday items and craft materials.

MAKE IT UP!

Besides real space travel, humans have come up with endless space-inspired sci-fi stories, films and TV shows, featuring imaginary spaceships and other futuristic inventions.

So remember, you don't have to stick to the exact models shown in this book – you can use your imagination. The instructions show you the basic modelling methods, tips and tricks, but you can explore your own out-of-this-world design ideas too. Come up with any new concepts you like. May the creative force be with you!

MAKER MATERIALS

The projects in this book have been designed to work using things you can find at home, such as disposable containers, packaging and basic art and craft equipment. If you don't have what you need, you can usually get it at a hobby or craft shop, supermarket or DIY store, or by ordering online. See page 31 for a list of useful sources.

Charity shops are a great place to look for old, cheap household items and materials, too.

CAN I USE THIS?

Before you start emptying the cupboards, make sure any containers or other household items you want to use are finished with, clean and you have permission to take them and make them into advanced space machinery. You're ready to launch!

WE HAVE LIFT-OFF!

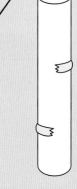

The space race began with rockets, and they're still essential for blasting off into orbit. Make your own and launch it into the air!

WHAT YOU NEED

- A strong narrow cardboard tube from a roll of foil or clingfilm
- White card
- Sticky tape (invisible if possible)
- A ruler
- A compass
- Scissors
- Marker pens
- Other decorations such as stickers or foil
- A large empty plastic fizzy drink bottle
- At least 45 cm of plastic tubing, about 2.5 cm wide
- Duct tape or other strong tape

You can buy plastic tubing at a DIY or hardware store – or use a piece of old garden hose.

1 Roll a piece of white card around your cardboard tube to make a cylinder and tape it together. It should fit closely around the tube, but be loose enough to slide off easily.

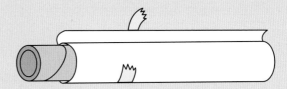

2 On a new piece of card, use the ruler to set your compass to draw a circle 11 cm across (5.5 cm radius). Then draw a second circle inside the first one, 10 cm across (5 cm radius). Cut out the outer circle.

3 Cut the circle in half and make cuts around the edge up to the outline of the inner circle. Curve it around to make a cone. Make sure the base is the same width as your cylinder. Sticky tape it together.

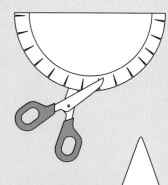

4 Fit the tabs into the top of your cylinder and sticky tape the cone to the cylinder well so that there are no gaps or holes. This is the rocket's nose cone.

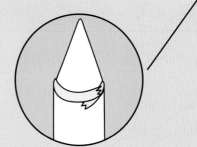

5 Draw three rocket fins on a piece of card. Cut them out and fold along the straight edge to make a tab. Tape them on to your rocket near the bottom.

6 Add windows, stripes, logos, lettering or other decorations to your rocket. (You could look at pictures of real rockets for inspiration.)

7 Line up the plastic tubing with the neck of the bottle and fix them together firmly with duct tape. Don't leave any gaps. Attach the other end of the tubing to the cardboard tube in the same way.

8 Fit your rocket on to the cardboard tube and point it upwards. It's best to do this outdoors. Make sure you aim away from people and animals. Now, stamp on the bottle to make the rocket fly!

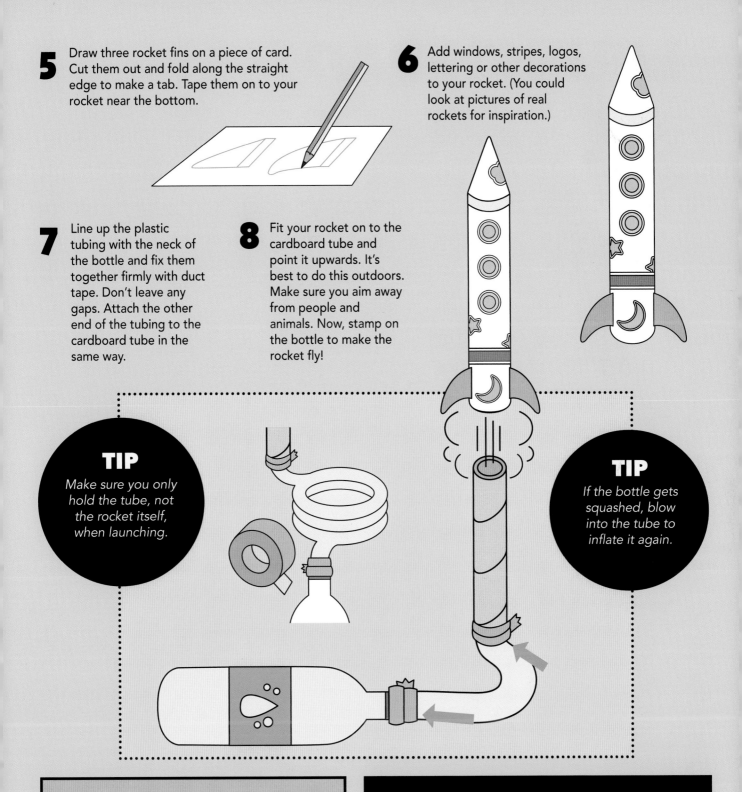

TIP
Make sure you only hold the tube, not the rocket itself, when launching.

TIP
If the bottle gets squashed, blow into the tube to inflate it again.

THE SCIENCE BIT!
This rocket works using air pressure. When you squeeze the bottle, you suddenly squash the air inside. It gets pushed along the tube and against the top of the rocket, forcing it upwards.

TAKE IT FURTHER ...
Make a target to fire your rocket at, such as a picture of the Moon or a planet stuck on to a wall.

LAUNCH PAD

All good space centres have a launch pad, with a platform and a launch tower to support rockets before take-off. Make your own using the rocket launcher from pages 6–7.

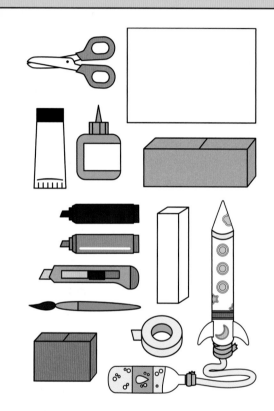

WHAT YOU NEED

- Rocket launcher and rocket from pages 6–7
- A low, wide cardboard box, such as a shoebox, for the platform
- A smaller, squarer cardboard box
- A long, narrow cardboard box for the tower
- Plain white paper, or white paint and a paintbrush
- Strong glue
- Sticky tape (invisible if possible)
- Scissors
- Marker pens, stickers and other decorations

1 Draw around the end of the rocket launcher tube on to the top of the small box, about 5 cm from one edge and centred left and right. With an adult's help, cut out the circle with a craft knife.

2 Make another hole the same way on the bottom of the small box. Make sure both holes line up. Use the rocket launcher tube to draw a circle 15 cm from one end of the platform box and centred left and right. Cut out this circle. Place the small box on top of the platform box to make sure the holes line up and the rocket launcher tube fits through all three holes.

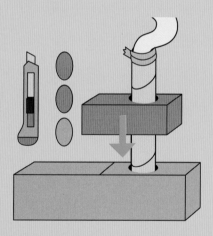

3 Neatly cut off the base of the platform box and mark a U-shape at one end, the same width as the rocket launcher tubing. Cut this out with the craft knife.

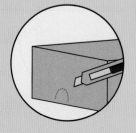 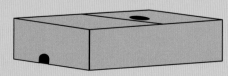

4 Now cover all three boxes with plain white paper or paint them white and leave to dry (unless they are white already). If using paper, cut holes where the holes in the boxes are.

5 Glue the boxes together using strong glue, with the holes in the small box and the platform box lined up. Stand the launch tower box at the end of the smaller box on the platform box. When the glue is dry, decorate the launch pad with grid patterns and logos.

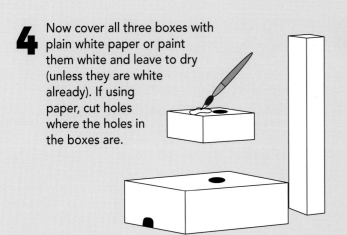

6 Push the rocket launcher tube up through the platform box and the small box, so that the tube stands upright next to the tower. Run the tubing out of the box through the U-shaped hole, so that the bottle lies next to the platform.

TIP
You can now launch your rocket from the launch pad.

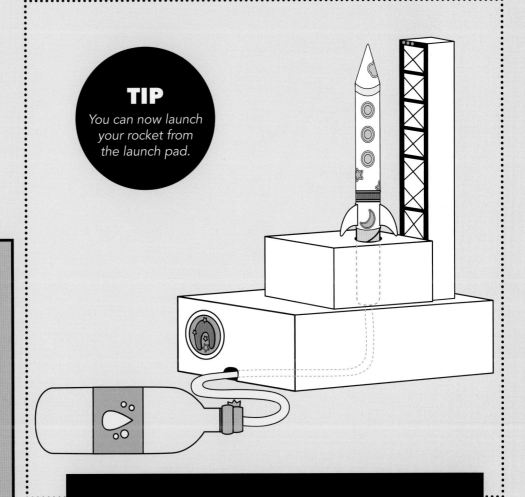

THE SCIENCE BIT!

At a real space centre, the launch tower is used to access the rocket to supply fuel, fit parts and let the astronauts enter the command module (see pages 10–11) at the top. As the rocket launches, the connections holding it in place are released.

TAKE IT FURTHER ...

You could use a very small box or cardboard tube to make an access gantry, linking the tower to the top of the rocket. But remember to move it out of the way when launching your rocket!

COMMAND MODULE

At the top of a crewed rocket, you'll see the small, cone-shaped command module. This is where the astronauts sit during take-off, and contains the instruments they need to control the mission.

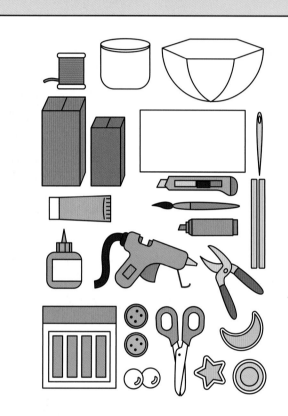

WHAT YOU NEED

- A large round plastic or paper bowl, such as a disposable salad bowl
- A smaller round plastic or paper bowl
- Small cardboard boxes
- Thick card
- A bradawl or large needle
- Garden wire and wire cutters, or a pipe cleaner
- Scissors and a craft knife
- Felt-tip and marker pens
- Two bendy straws
- Strong glue or a glue gun
- Silver or grey paint and a paintbrush
- White PVA glue
- Beads, buttons, lids, straws or other small objects
- Plain stickers
- Sticky tack

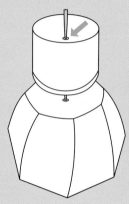

1 Use the bradawl or needle to make a hole in the middle of the base of each bowl. Glue the small bowl on top of the larger one.

2 Fold the pipe cleaner, or a piece of wire about 30 cm long, in half to make a loop. Push the ends through both bowls from the top, leaving the loop sticking out. Inside the larger bowl, bend the ends over to hold the wire in place.

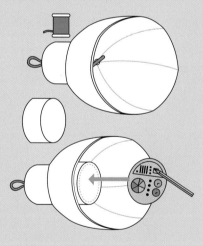

3 Cut off part of a small cardboard box. Glue it inside the larger bowl to make a control panel. Cut a piece of card the same size as the panel. Draw controls and buttons on it and stick it on.

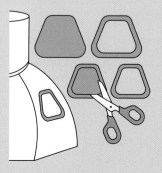

4 With a marker, draw an entry hatch and smaller windows on the larger bowl. Carefully cut them out. Draw around the cut-out shapes on to thick card. Cut out a frame for each one. Glue the frames around the holes.

5 For the entry hatch, cut out a door shape the same size as the frame around the entry hatch. Cut a smaller strip of card and glue it to the bowl above the entry hatch frame.

6 Draw around the large bowl on to thick card. Cut out the shape to make a base. Cut two seat shapes from the corners of small cardboard boxes, and glue them to the middle of the base.

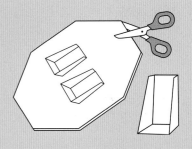

7 Glue objects such as buttons, beads, lids and pieces of straw on to the module to make controls and instruments. When they're dry, paint the module, the base and the hatch door with grey or silver paint, mixed with an equal amount of white PVA glue to help it stick. Leave to dry.

8 Cut the ends off the straws, leaving about 1 cm on each side of the bendy sections. Glue one end of each straw to the hatch door and the other ends to the strip above the door, so that it can open and close.

9 Finally, attach the base to the module with sticky tack. You can hang the module up using the loop on top.

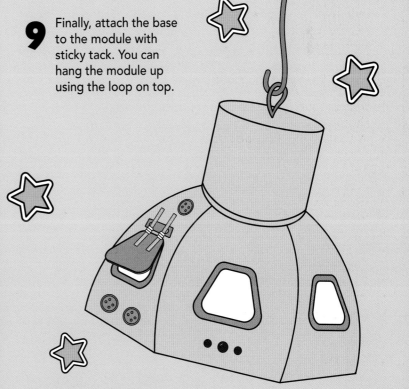

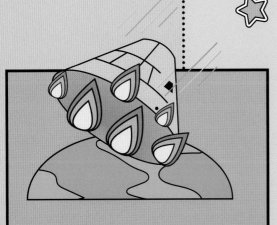

THE SCIENCE BIT!

After separating from the rocket, the command module brings the astronauts back to Earth. It gets very hot as it speeds through the atmosphere, so real-life modules have a thick heat shield.

PARACHUTE DESCENT

As a command module approaches Earth's surface it deploys its parachutes. They slow it down before landing, so the astronauts don't hit the ground too hard. (It's still a pretty bumpy experience, though!)

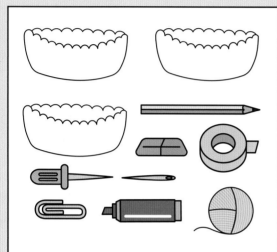

WHAT YOU NEED

- Three large, round paper cake tin liners
- A red marker pen
- A bradawl or large needle
- An eraser
- A pencil
- Strong tape, such as duct tape
- String or strong sewing thread
- A large paper clip

If you can't find cake tin liners, you can try making parachutes using a large circle of tissue paper, or thin plastic from a white plastic bag or bin liner.

1 Return-module parachutes are usually patterned red and white. Use the red marker pen to draw stripes around the edge of one of the cake tin liners and a large red circle on top – or make up your own design.

2 Stick two small pieces of strong tape in the middle of the parachute, one on the top and one on the inside. Cut four small strips of strong tape, and stick them at equally spaced points around the edge of the parachute, wrapping them over the edge.

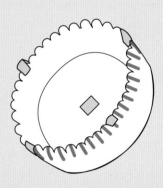

3 Use the bradawl or needle to make holes through all five pieces of tape. When pushing the sharp tip through, hold the eraser on the other side for it to stick into. Make the hole in the top bigger than the others by pushing the pencil through it too.

4 Cut two equal pieces of string, each about 80 cm long. Tie to the parachute by knotting the four ends into the holes around the edge.

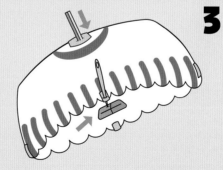

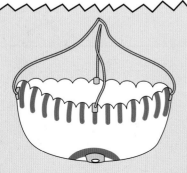

5 Now repeat the whole process for the other two cake liners, so that you have three parachutes. (Or, if your module is quite small, it might only need one or two.)

6 Lie all the parachutes down side by side. Find the middle point of each string. Fold it and tie a knot leaving a small loop. Hook all the strings from all the parachutes into one end of the large paper clip.

7 Hook the other end of the paper clip into the loop on top of the command module. It's now ready to descend. You could try (carefully!) dropping it over the banister of a staircase, or just hang it up as a model from the command module loop.

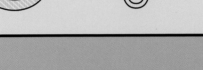

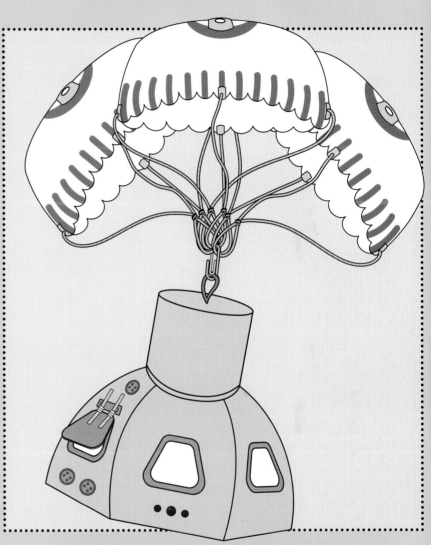

THE SCIENCE BIT!

Parachutes slow things down using air resistance. As air flows around and into the parachute, it pushes the parachute upwards, working against gravity. The hole in the top of the parachute lets a little air through, helping to keep it upright instead of flipping over.

TAKE IT FURTHER ...

Astronauts also do parachute training so that they can escape from a malfunctioning spacecraft.
For an emergency escape parachute, make a single parachute as above, and hook the two loops of string under an astronaut figure's arms.

SPACE SATELLITE

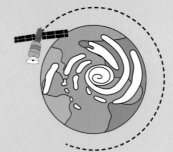

A satellite is an object that orbits around a larger object in space. For example, our Moon is a natural satellite. Artificial satellites are a type of spacecraft, sent into orbit to do a job, such as taking photos of Earth.

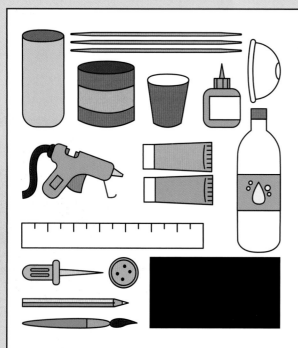

WHAT YOU NEED

- Tube-shaped and cone-shaped containers
- A plastic dome from a slushy cup, or an empty fizzy drink bottle
- A bradawl or large needle
- Strong glue or a glue gun
- Wooden skewers
- Thick black card
- A silver marker or white pencil
- A ruler
- A black bead, button or small pen lid
- Craft paints
- White PVA glue
- Paintbrushes

1 Design your satellite by arranging your boxes and containers into the shape you want. Many satellites are made of a sequence of tube-like shapes.

2 Use the bradawl or large needle to make holes through the middle of each container. Push a wooden skewer through them to string them together. Glue them together. Leave about 2 cm of skewer sticking out at each end.

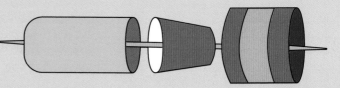

3 Make holes through the width of one of the containers, and push another skewer through them so that there are equal amounts of skewer sticking out on each side.

4 Paint the satellite body using paint mixed with an equal amount of white PVA glue. Satellites are usually a combination of white, black, silver, gold and grey, but you can use other colours if you like. Each part can be a different colour.

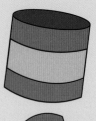

5 If you don't have a slushy cup lid to make a satellite dish, draw around a round object such as a paper cup on to the curved part of a plastic bottle. Cut out the dish shape and make a hole in the middle. Paint the dish with white paint mixed with PVA glue.

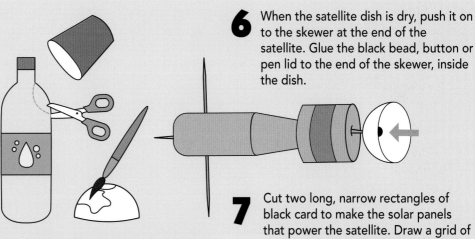

6 When the satellite dish is dry, push it on to the skewer at the end of the satellite. Glue the black bead, button or pen lid to the end of the skewer, inside the dish.

7 Cut two long, narrow rectangles of black card to make the solar panels that power the satellite. Draw a grid of lines on them using a ruler and a silver marker or white pencil (see left).

8 Carefully glue the solar panels to the pieces of skewer on the sides of the satellite, lining up the skewer with the centre of each panel.

THE SCIENCE BIT!

Satellites do all kinds of useful things. Some carry telescopes for studying the stars. Others transmit phone and GPS (Global Positioning System) signals around the world, or take photos and measurements of Earth to forecast the weather or detect global warming.

TIP

To display the satellite, tie a piece of sewing thread to it and hang it up safely with an adult's help.

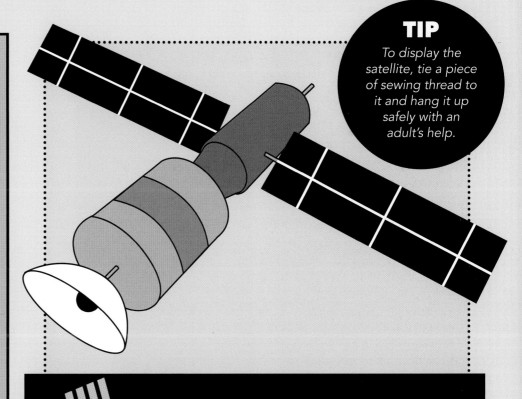

TAKE IT FURTHER ...

The biggest satellites are space stations, where astronauts can stay and live for weeks or months at a time. You could research what they look like and try building one. You'll need a LOT of tubes!

HUMAN GYROSCOPE

A human what? A human gyroscope, or aerotrim, is a strange-looking exercise machine. It's used to train astronauts to keep their balance and cope with dizziness during their space missions in microgravity. Every space centre should have one!

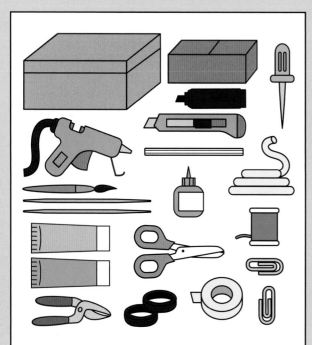

WHAT YOU NEED

- A strong cardboard box, such as a shoebox
- 2 m of plastic tubing, about 1 cm wide
- A small cardboard box
- Scissors and a craft knife
- Strong glue or a glue gun
- Strong, sticky tape (invisible if possible)
- A marker pen
- A bradawl or large needle
- Metal paper clips or garden wire
- Small pliers
- An empty ink tube from a ballpoint pen
- Wooden skewers
- Black sewing elastic or old hairbands
- Felt tip pens or paints and paintbrushes
- An astronaut figure (or other small toy)

You can find plastic tubing at a DIY store, or sometimes at a kitchen store.

1 Mark a line around the base of your shoebox, about 3 cm from the bottom. On both lengths, in the middle, mark a triangle up to the top of the box.
Cut out this shape to make a frame for your gyroscope. Decorate or paint it.

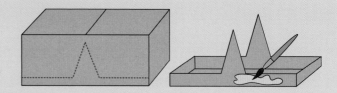

2 Loop the tubing into a ring almost the same width as the distance between the two triangles. Mark where the tubing meets. Cut it off neatly with scissors.

3 Glue the ends of the tubing together and fix with some sticky tape. Make another, smaller ring the same way. It should fit inside the first ring with a little space to spare.

4 Put one ring inside the other and mark them on opposite sides. At these points, use the bradawl or needle to make holes through both rings, from the outer edge to the inner edge.

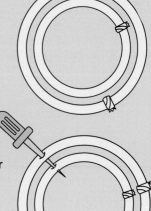

5 Use the scissors or craft knife to cut small pieces off the empty ink tube. Open out a paper clip or cut a short piece of wire. Thread it through the outer ring, then a piece of ink tube, then the inner ring.

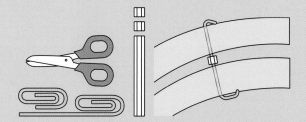

6 Trim and bend the ends of the wire to hold them in place. Do the same on the other side of the rings. They should now be linked together, but able to spin independently.

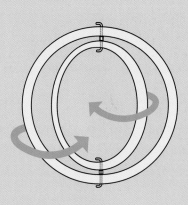

7 Mark the larger ring half way between the points where it connects to the inner ring. Make holes through it with a bradawl or needle and make holes at the top of the triangles in the frame. As before, use wire and pieces of ink tube to connect the outer ring to the frame so that it can spin.

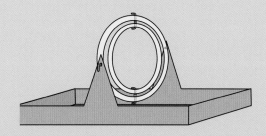

8 Mark and cut a chair shape from the small cardboard box. Cut two pieces of wooden skewer the width of the smaller ring, and tape them to the sides of the chair. Paint the chair and skewers and leave to dry. Fit the skewers into the smaller ring by making small holes in the inside of the ring and pushing the skewers into them.

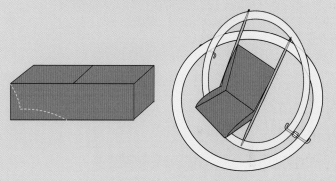

9 Tie or glue black elastic or hairbands to the skewers and chair to make stretchy straps (make holes in the chair to loop elastic through if necessary). You can now sit an astronaut figure in the chair and spin the rings to give him or her a workout!

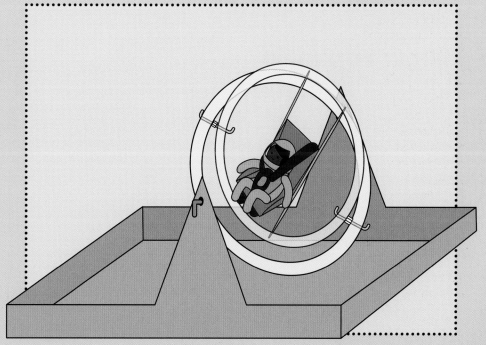

PASSENGER SPACESHIP

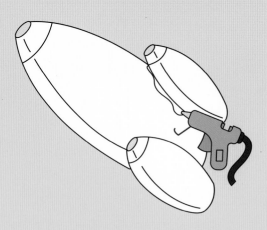

In the future, you'll be able to take holidays in space …
as long as you can afford a flight on a super-high-tech
passenger spaceship, that is! Space tourism firms are
already building the first models, but as time goes on,
they'll need new designs. What will yours look like?

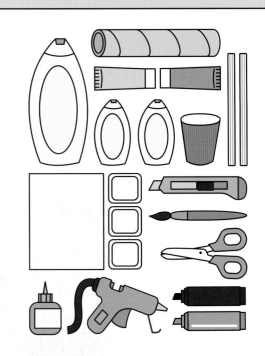

WHAT YOU NEED

- Empty plastic bottles, containers and
  packaging with interesting, space-age
  shapes, such as cones, triangles, or
  curved, pointy nozzles
- Cardboard tubes
- Straws
- Thick card
- Scissors and a craft knife
- Craft paints
- Paintbrushes
- White PVA glue
- Strong glue or a glue gun
- Plain stickers
- Felt-tip pens and metallic markers

1 Wash out your containers or bottles and peel or soak off
any labels. Choose a bottle or container to make the main
body of your spaceship. If you want to attach different
parts or shapes together, do this first, using strong glue or
a glue gun.

2 You can leave the containers unpainted (especially if
they're white, gold or silver) or paint them with paints
mixed with an equal amount of white PVA glue to help
them stick. White, black, blue and metallic colours often
feature on futuristic spaceships.

3 To make wings, draw a large, wide two-wing shape on to
thick card. Cut it out and paint it if you want to. When it's
dry, glue it to your spaceship body.

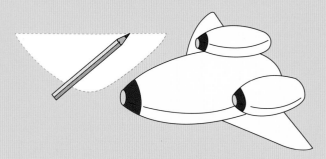

4 To make rocket thrusters, use cone-shaped
containers, such as small dessert pots. Cut a piece of
cardboard tube to fit inside each pot. Paint the pots
and tubes if necessary. When they're dry, glue the
tubes inside the pots.

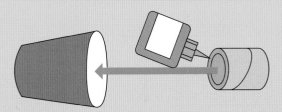

5 Cut the straws into seven short pieces, slightly longer than the thrusters. Line them up and tape them together to make a bundle. Paint it if you like. Glue it inside a thruster. Repeat for the other thrusters. Glue the thrusters on to the back of the spaceship.

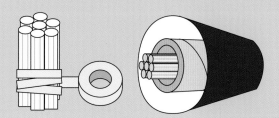

6 Draw windows and designs such as logos and lettering on to plain stickers. Stick them on to your spaceship. (This makes it easy to start again if you go wrong.)

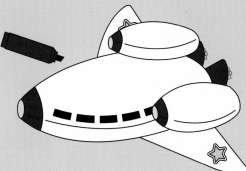

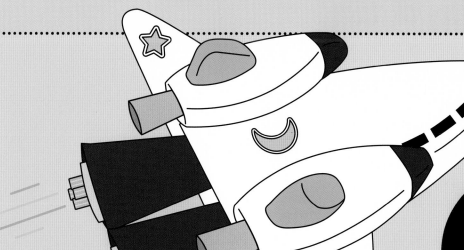

TIP
Add more lids, buttons or small objects to make cockpits, if you like.

THE SCIENCE BIT!
It's tricky to develop passenger spacecraft, as they have to be able to go to space carrying a large number of people, return safely and be used again, similar to an airliner. They are usually designed to be carried into space by a separate aircraft or rocket, then released.

TAKE IT FURTHER ...
In sci-fi movies and TV shows, people spend years on huge, intergalactic spaceships with room for hundreds of passengers. Can you design and make one of those?

MARS ROVER

Mars is one of our closest planets and the one we've explored more than any other. Although no humans have yet gone to Mars, we've sent several robotic rovers there. Controlled from Earth, they land on Mars and set out to explore, take photos, collect samples, and send back information about what they find.

Our model rover is similar to the Mars Curiosity Rover, but you can design yours however you like.

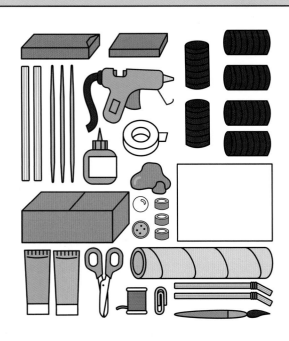

WHAT YOU NEED

- A flattish cardboard box, such as a chocolate box
- A smaller, narrower flat box
- Four or six large, black hair rollers
- Straws
- Wooden skewers
- Modelling clay
- Strong sticky tape (invisible if possible)
- Strong glue or a glue gun
- Thick card
- Smaller boxes and cardboard tubes
- Bead, buttons, lids and other small household items
- Metal paper clips or garden wire
- Two bendy straws
- Craft paints
- Paintbrushes
- White PVA glue

1 Glue the two flat boxes together, so that the small one is positioned in the middle of the large one.

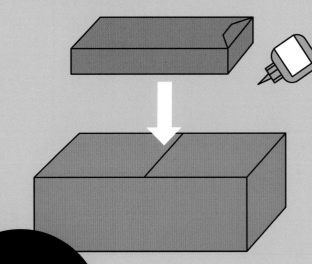

Hair rollers make great rover wheels, but if you can't get them, you could use pieces of cardboard tube instead.

2 Cut two pieces of straw (if you want four wheels) or three pieces (if you want six wheels) the same width as the small box. Tape them to the underneath of the smaller box, spacing them out evenly. Slide a wooden skewer through each straw to make the axles.

3 Roll balls of modelling clay to the right size to fit tightly inside your hair rollers or cardboard wheels. Push them inside, then push the skewers into the clay. If the wheels stick out too far, take them off and shorten the skewers.

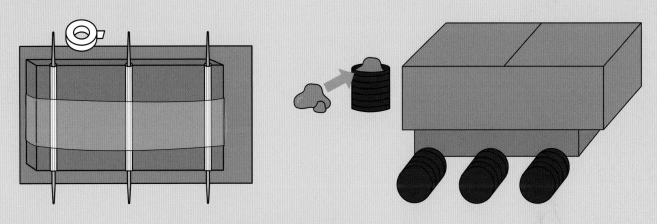

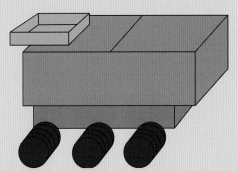

4 Cut the base off a smaller box, or use a small box lid, to make a tray-like shape. Glue this to the top of the rover at the back, partly sticking out.

5 If you want to, you can now paint the basic rover body, before adding the other parts. Real rovers usually have a combination of black, silver, grey and white parts. Mix your paints with an equal amount of PVA glue before using them to help them stick.

Turn the page to continue.

TAKE IT FURTHER ...

Our model has fixed wheels, but on a real rover, they can turn in all directions, and even move up and down to get over obstacles. How would you make wheels that can do this?

6 Laser and camera head

To create the laser and camera head you need a small, narrow tube and a small, rectangular box. Draw around the end of the tube on to the box. Cut out the circle and fit the tube into the box. Glue card circles or buttons of different sizes to the front of the box. Paint the camera if you like and leave to dry. Make a hole in the rover and push the tube through it. Glue in place.

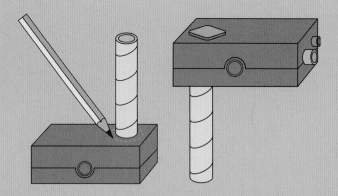

The cameras take photos of the surroundings, helping the rover to plan its route. The laser blasts rocks to heat them up and turn them into gases. Sensors then detect the gases to figure out what the rocks are made of.

7 Nuclear heat battery

Cut a cardboard tube to fit inside the box on the back of the rover or make a tube by rolling up a piece of card. Cut four rectangles of card the same length as the tube. Cut slits half way along one side of the tube and half way along each card rectangle. Slot the rectangles into the tube to make the battery. Glue it into the box on the rover.

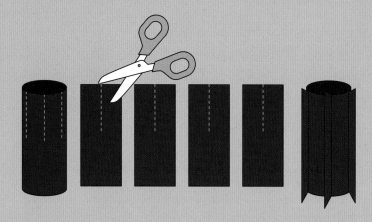

The nuclear heat battery uses radioactive chemicals to generate electricity to power the rover, as a well as heat to keep it warm enough to work in the freezing temperatures of Mars.

8 Robot arm

Make a cut into the short end of a bendy straw. Carefully push it into the short end of the second bendy straw to make an arm with two joints. Trim off the longer ends. Fit one end into a narrow pen lid or other small tube.

Make a claw from a strip of thick card bent into a U-shape. Make a hole in the middle with a sharp pencil and push it on to the pen lid or tube on the end of the straw. Glue another pen lid to the side of the rover, facing upwards. Stand the other end of the straw in it, so that the robot arm can rotate freely.

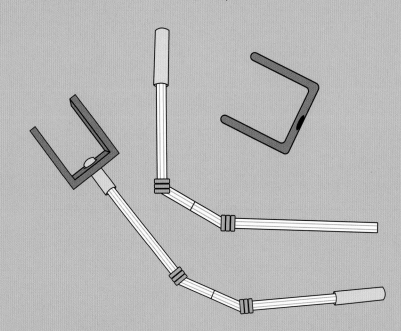

9 Weather station

Take a small box and glue on hi-tech-looking buttons, beads, pieces of straw or other interesting objects to make weather instruments. Make a two-pronged antenna from wire or a paper clip. Thread the ends through a two-holed button, then glue the button on to the box. Paint the weather station if you like, then glue it to the top of the rover.

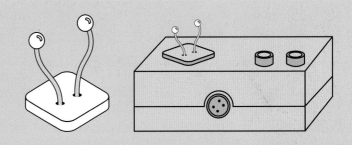

10 More bits and bobs

Take a look at pictures of real Mars rovers on the Internet and add any other objects you like to make more instruments, sensors and tools. Use stickers or marker pens to add finishing touches such as a logo or lettering.

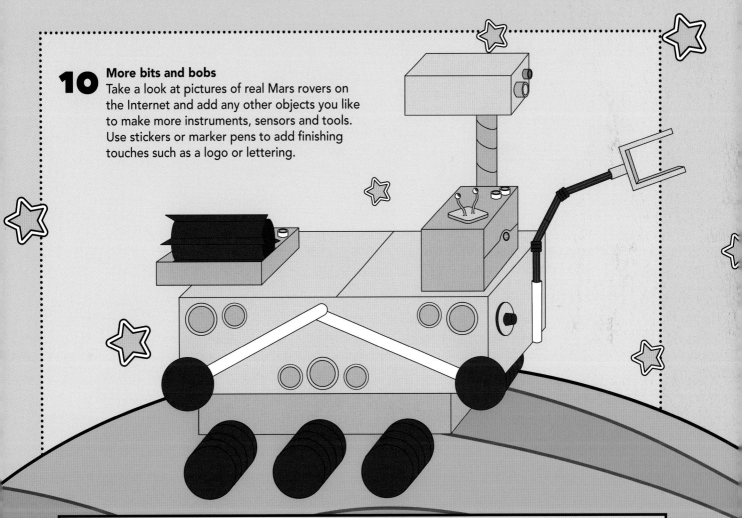

THE SCIENCE BIT!

Mars rovers can collect samples of soil and rock, analyse them, then send their findings back to Earth in the form of radio signals. This can reveal what Mars is made of, and how much water it has on it. It could even help us discover if there is any form of life on Mars.

PLANETARIUM PROJECTOR

A planetarium is a map of the night sky displayed on the inside of a special theatre. Using this projector, you can make a room at home into a planetarium – the perfect backdrop for your space centre!

WHAT YOU NEED

- A round breakfast bowl or small mixing bowl
- Clingfilm
- Baby oil or bath oil
- Newspaper
- White PVA glue
- An old plastic container or paper cup
- A tablespoon
- A large piece of cardboard
- Scissors
- Masking tape
- Black paint and a paint brush
- A bradawl or large needle
- An eraser
- A silver marker or white pencil
- A small, bright, single LED torch
- Modelling clay or sticky tack
- A sheet of black card

1 Cover the bowl with a layer of clingfilm. Rub a small amount of baby oil or bath oil over it to prevent sticking. Pour about 2–3 cm of PVA glue into the container. Stir in a few tablespoons of water.

2 Tear your newspaper into 2 cm wide strips. One at a time, dip them in the glue mixture. Spread them over the surface of the bowl. Keep adding strips until the bowl is covered with about five layers. This process is called papier mâché. Leave to dry overnight.

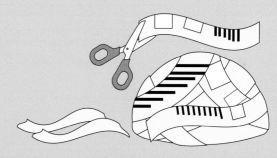

3 When it's dry, carefully pull the paper dome off the bowl and remove the clingfilm. Cut out a long strip of cardboard, about 5 cm wide, and 3.5 times as long as the width of your paper dome.

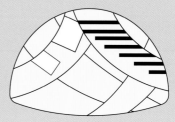

5 cm

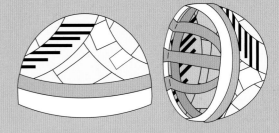

4 Wrap the cardboard strip around the base of your dome, overlapping it slightly. Glue or tape the ends of the strip together. Use masking tape to attach the dome to the strip, sealing the join tightly inside and outside.

5 Mix black paint with an equal amount of PVA glue. Paint the dome and the strip black all over, inside and outside. Leave to dry, propped up slightly so that air can get in.

6 Using a book or the Internet, find a simple, circular map of the night sky, showing several constellations. Print it out or copy it on to paper, making the circle slightly larger than your dome.

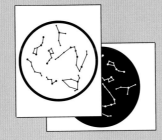

8 Roll a lump of modelling clay or sticky tack into a ball. Press it on to the middle of your black card. Push the torch into it so that it points upwards.

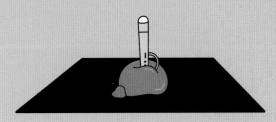

7 Make holes through the star dots on the paper with the bradawl or needle. Carefully hold the paper over your dome and use a silver marker or white pencil to mark the black dome surface through the holes.

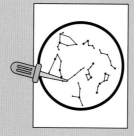

9 Make a hole through each dot on the dome. As you push the bradawl or needle through, hold the eraser on the other side for it to stick into. When it's finished, switch on the torch and place the dome over it. Turn off the lights to see the stars and constellations!

THE SCIENCE BIT!

Stars in the night sky seem to form patterns, which we see as constellations or familiar shapes. In fact, some of the stars in a constellation are much further away than others. They just look as if they form a group when viewed from Earth.

SPACE CENTRE

Make a space centre to keep all your models on. Space centres are BIG, as they need a large area for launching spacecraft, as well as hangars for keeping them in, astronaut training equipment, office buildings and control towers. Look at aerial photos of real space centres and spaceports on the Internet for inspiration.

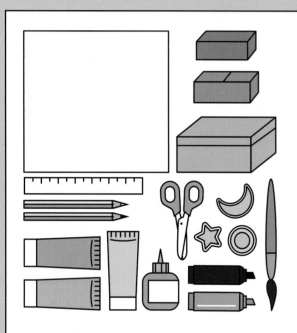

WHAT YOU NEED

- A very big piece of cardboard*
- Cardboard boxes and tubes of different sizes
- Scissors
- Pencils and a ruler
- Marker and felt-tip pens
- Craft paints and paintbrushes
- White PVA glue
- Stickers

*You could use packaging cardboard from a large appliance, such as a washing machine. If you can't find one, tape several smaller pieces of cardboard together.

1 Start by cutting your cardboard into a circle, hexagon or whatever shape you like. Mark a large launch area in the middle to put the rocket launcher from pages 8–9.

2 Mark roads leading from the launch area out to the edges of the space centre and add a little road around the edge too.

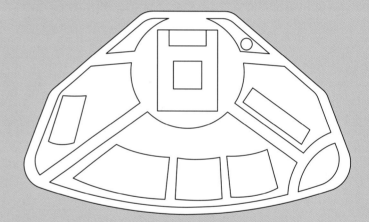

3 Paint or colour in the space centre base before adding the buildings. In real space centres, the roads and launch area are usually white or pale grey, with green grass in between.

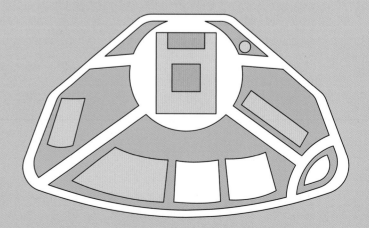

4 Now you can make the buildings. To make a hangar, use a large cardboard box that's big enough to fit one of your models, such as the spaceship or rover, inside. Cut a large doorway in the front of the box. Paint the box in cool colours.

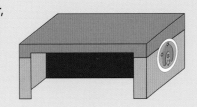

5 For control towers, use tall tube-shaped containers. Paint them white and add some windows near the top. You could also add a clear round plastic bowl on top to make a viewing dome.

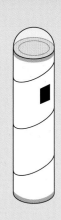

6 For office and training buildings, choose low, rectangular boxes. Paint them white and add dark windows. Arrange all your buildings around the space centre, next to the roads.

7 Add the finishing touches by drawing logos and lettering on stickers and adding them to the buildings. You could use a matching name and logo on all your models.

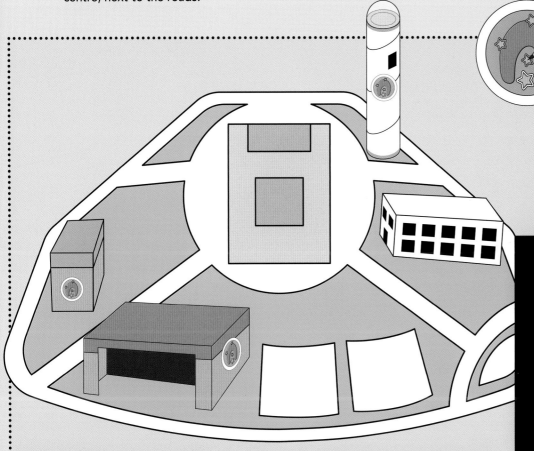

THE SCIENCE BIT!

Real space centres are often built in remote places, well away from city centres and homes. That's because launching rockets is incredibly loud and can sometimes go wrong, leading to crashes or explosions.

TIP

You might not be able to fit all of your models on to your space centre, especially if you've made them quite big. Instead, you could hang up some of the flying spacecraft. Ask an adult to help you attach thread to the models and fix them to the ceiling for you.

AND HERE IS YOUR FINISHED SPACE CENTRE!

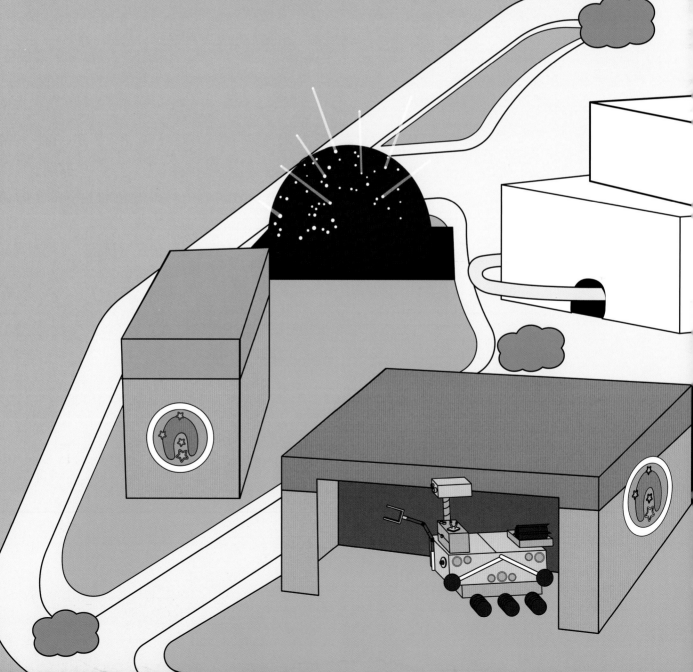

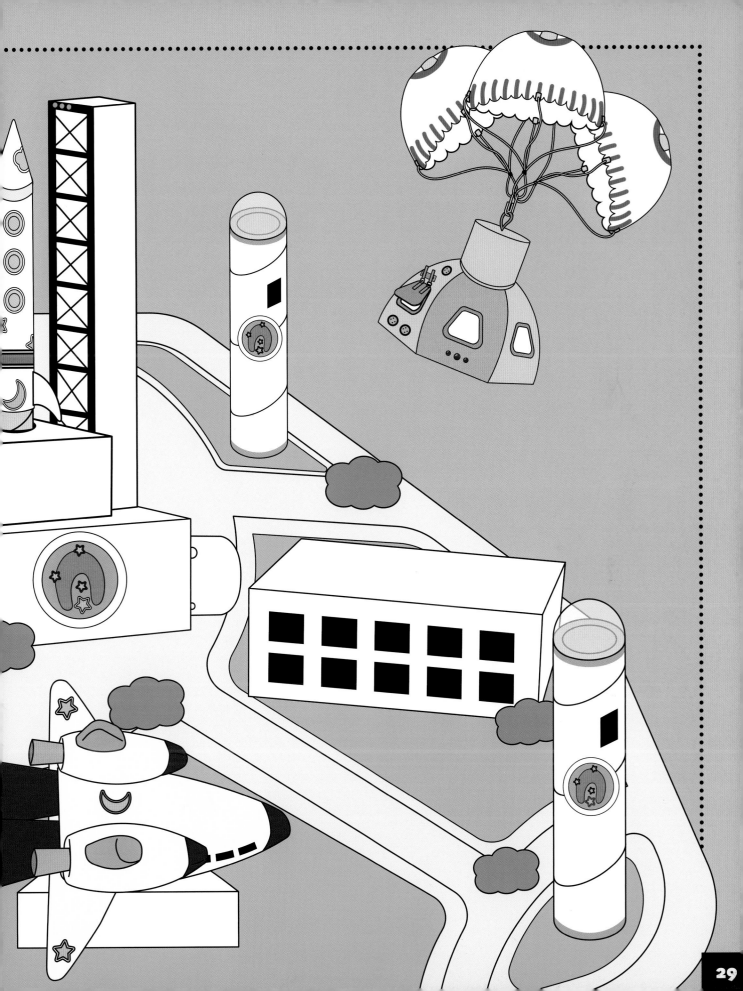

GLOSSARY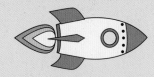

Aerotrim A large gyroscope that a human can sit inside, used for training astronauts.

Air pressure A force caused by air pushing against something.

Air resistance A force caused by air pushing against something that is moving through it.

Astronaut Someone who is trained to travel into space. Those trained by Russia's space agency are known as Cosmonauts.

Atmosphere The layer of gases surrounding Earth or another planet.

Bradawl A sharp, pointed tool for making neat holes.

Command module The part of a spacecraft that carries the crew and contains the control equipment.

Constellation A group of stars that appear from Earth to form a pattern or shape.

Gantry A bridge-like structure that connects to a rocket on the launch pad, allowing astronauts and supplies to enter.

Global warming A gradual increase in the average temperature of Earth's surface and atmosphere.

Glue gun A gun-shaped electric tool that heats up and applies strong glue.

GPS Short for Global Positioning System, a system of satellites and receivers that allow people to pinpoint where they are on Earth's surface.

Gyroscope A device containing a wheel that spins inside a frame that can also rotate.

Hangar A building with a large space inside for keeping aircraft or spacecraft in.

Heat shield A covering or layer on the outside of a spacecraft that protects it from the build-up of heat during re-entry into the atmosphere.

Intergalactic Able to travel or transmit between different galaxies.

Laser A device that sends out a narrow, powerful beam of light.

Launch pad An area or platform that a rocket stands on before being launched.

LED Short for Light-Emitting Diode, a type of small, bright electric light.

Orbit To circle around a larger object in space.

Radioactive Giving out energy in the form of rays or moving particles.

Radius The length of a straight line joining the centre of a circle to its edge.

Rover A robot vehicle used to explore the surface of a planet, moon or other space object.

Satellite Something that orbits around a planet or other space object. Artificial satellites orbit Earth to do useful tasks.

Sci-fi Short for Science Fiction, meaning fictional stories about space, the future or futuristic technology.

Space mission A planned journey into space for a particular purpose.

Space station A large satellite spacecraft where astronauts can live and work in space.

Space tourism Travelling into space for a fun experience or holiday, instead of as a job.

Wire clippers A tool shaped like a pair of pliers, but with sharp blades for cutting wire.

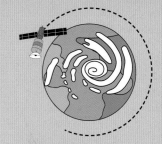

FURTHER INFORMATION

WHERE TO GET MATERIALS

Everyday items
You'll probably have some everyday items and craft materials at home already, such as food wrap, pens, foil, paper clips, clingfilm, string, paper and card, sticky tape, glue and scissors.

Recycling
Old packaging that's going to be thrown away or recycled is a great source of making materials – such as cardboard boxes, plastic bottles, yoghurt pots, ice cream tubs, cardboard tubes, magazines, old wrapping paper and newspaper.

Specialist shops
Hobby and craft shops, sewing shops, art shops, garden centres and DIY stores could be useful for things like a craft knife and a glue gun, modelling clay, silver paint, silver and black card, plastic tubing, beads and buttons. If you don't have the shop you need near you, ask an adult to help you look for online shops, such as Hobbycraft.

Charity shops
It's always a good idea to check charity shops when you can, as they often have all kinds of handy household items and craft materials at very low prices.

BOOKS

Space Atlas
by Tom Jackson
QED, 2018

Space Academy: How to fly Spacecraft Step by Step
by Dorling Kindersley
Dorling Kindersley, 2015

Dr Maggie's Grand Tour of the Solar System
by Dr Maggie Aderin-Pocock
Buster Books, 2019

Junk Modelling
By Annalees Lim
Wayland, 2016

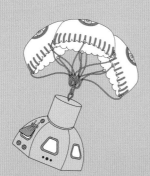

WEBSITES

PNASA SpacePlace Crafts
https://spaceplace.nasa.gov/menu/do/
Fun space things to make and do from NASA.

PBS Design Squad
https://pbskids.org/designsquad/
Lots of brilliant design and build challenges.

DIY
https://diy.org/
An online maker community for kids.

Parents.com Arts & Crafts
https://www.parents.com/fun/arts-crafts/?page=1
Maker projects, instructions and videos.

Kiwico DIY page
https://www.kiwico.com/diy/
Fun and easy maker ideas.

INDEX